Fragments of a Stolen Life:

Reclaiming My Name, My Legacy, and My Truth

Lata Leare Obama

Dedication

I thank God and my ancestors for blessing me on my publication journey and my overall safekeeping. I would also like to dedicate this book to myself, my biological parents (especially my *Abu*, Father in Arabic), my children, my grandchildren, my tribe, and my loved ones who loyally love me.

A special mention to my sister from another mister, Tanisha Frame: thank you for walking with and beside me during my darkest hours. This project has been coming for a long time, and in the words of Diana Ross, "I'm coming out. I want the world to know. Got to let it show." I was born Lata Leare Obama.

Thank you, Momma Tammie, for telling me the truth and for your heartfelt apologies; I know you always wanted to become a published author, and this one is for us! This lotus has blossomed through all of the cracks.

Acknowledgment

I thank Allah and all of my guardian angels for keeping me safe. This journey is not for the weak at heart; it has been tumultuous!

I want to express my deepest gratitude to all of my supporters, known and unbeknownst to me. This would include my biological parents; thank you both for creating me and may you forever be blessed for blessing me to be born. My biological eldest child, who was taken from me and given up for adoption without my consent- I love you, and I pray we are reunited soon. All of my biological children after her. You all have motivated me in unspeakable ways— A huge thank you to my publishing team, Brooklyn Publishers, especially Liam Cooper for all his help. Thank you for believing in me and my project, for your dedicated assistance in publishing my book, and for helping me complete my story in written format. Thank you to everyone who has prayed for me and supported my truth. A special thanks to my non-supporters (haters); you have been my motivators in completing this task of speaking up for and reclaiming all that was stolen from me.

About the Author

Lata Leare is a proud Kansan, born and raised in Wichita, Kansas. I was born at St. Francis Hospital with my signature sandy brown hair, embodying the warmth and resilience of my homegrown roots. A lifelong learner and dedicated professional, I'm a proud alumni of Wichita State University (WSU) and Baker University, where I earned my Bachelor of Arts (WSU) Master's in Business Administration, solidifying my passion for leadership and service.

Throughout my life, I have lived in Wichita, Kansas; Fort Worth and Arlington, Texas; and the vibrant Atlanta, Georgia, metropolitan area, gaining diverse perspectives that have shaped my advocacy work. As a devoted mother and grandmother—affectionately called "GG" and "Grandma Too Sweet"—I treasure family and the values of compassion and integrity.

I'm deeply committed to justice. I dedicate my time to helping others advocate for their rights and seek fairness in their lives. Whether through professional endeavors or personal passions, I have unwavering support for those in need.

I currently reside in my beloved Wichita, Kansas, and embrace my identity as a true Kansan. I cherish the opportunity to give back to my community while championing the causes closest to my heart.

Preface

In channeling my biological father's energy, *"Cream always rises to the top."* I'm crème de la crème!

The old me, Lata Leare Tomlinson, is dead and gone. The reclaimed me, Lata Leare Obama, is living life on purpose and with purpose. I have accomplished many things in my lifetime, including graduating from Wichita State University and Baker University with an MBA. I previously worked as an Accountant and held other positions in corporate America. I am a certified paralegal and completed my paralegal certification at the Emory Continuing Education Center in Atlanta, Georgia. I currently advocate for those with special needs to help the families advocate for their rights and to help hold educational institutions to the federal guidelines of IEPs (individual education plans) and 504 plans. I have recently relocated back to Wichita, Kansas, where I am a proud-born native.

Contents

Introduction

I have always felt like something was missing in my life, as if a piece of me had been hidden away, locked behind a door, and I didn't have the key to it. Growing up, I lived with a family who adopted me when I was young. From the outside, they looked perfect—a house in a good neighborhood, stability, and the appearance of a caring environment. But the truth is that as I grew older, I realized that I had to fight for love every day, and even then, it rarely came.

My adoptive parents were not the loving figures they appeared to be. Behind closed doors, I faced years of abuse—physical, emotional, and psychological. Every time I was told I wasn't good enough, every time I was made to feel small, I retreated further into myself. There were nights I cried myself to sleep, wondering what I had done to deserve such treatment. I didn't realize then that it wasn't about me at all—it was about them, their brokenness, and their inability to love. But try explaining that to a child who wants to be held and told that everything will be okay.

By the time I was a teenager, I was living in survival mode. I got used to the idea that no one was coming to save me. I had to save myself. And while I didn't have the words for it back then, that's where my strength started to build. I didn't know it yet, but those years of abuse would become the foundation of my resilience—the part of me that would never break or fold, no matter how hard life got.

But the abuse wasn't the only secret I had to uncover. As I entered adulthood, I stumbled upon something that shook me: Barack Obama Jr. was my biological father. Imagine hearing something like that—a figure known worldwide, someone you've seen on TV giving powerful speeches and leading a country, someone who seemed so far removed from your reality and somehow connected to your very existence.

At first, I didn't believe it. It sounded like a bad dream or some wild conspiracy theory. But as I dug deeper, the pieces started to come together. There were documents, letters, and old photos that connected the dots. The more I discovered, the more undeniable it became. This revelation was both empowering and terrifying. On one hand, I finally had an answer to a question I hadn't even known I was asking: Who am I? But on the other hand, this opened up a world of emotions and challenges I hadn't anticipated.

During this time, I also found my faith. Growing up, I had been exposed to many different religions and belief systems, but none of them spoke to me in the way that Islam did. My conversion to Islam was a profoundly personal decision, one that brought me a sense of peace I had never experienced before. Islam taught me about forgiveness, about how to let go of the anger and bitterness that had built up inside me over the years.

In a world that felt chaotic and unjust, my faith gave me a grounding point. Islam isn't just a religion; it's a way of life. It gave me the tools I needed to heal, not just spiritually but emotionally. The act of prayer, the community, and the teachings all helped me find the strength to forgive—not just the people who had hurt me but also myself. I had been carrying so much guilt for so many years, blaming myself for things that were never my fault to begin with. Islam helped me release that weight.

It wasn't easy—forgiveness never is—but I knew that if I didn't let go of the pain, it would continue to hold power over me. A quote from the Qur'an has always stuck with me: *"So be patient. Indeed, the promise of Allah is truth."* That became my mantra during the darkest times of my life. I had to remind myself that no matter how bad things seemed, there was always hope, always light at the end of the tunnel.

The truth about my father was just one part of my journey, but it was a catalyst for so much more. It forced me to confront the past, heal from the trauma, and finally step into the person I was always meant to be. Today, I stand tall, not just as the daughter of a former president but as Lata Leare— the woman who refused to be broken.

Chapter 1: True Identity Revealed

Nothing is more important than knowing who you are, where you came from, and what your life's purpose is. It's something I've thought about a lot in my life. Growing up, I always felt a sense of confusion about who I was and where I belonged. I was told many stories about my origins, but none of them ever truly fit. The truth, however, always has a way of coming to the surface. I was born Lata Leare Obama, and that's not just a belief; it's a matter of fact supported by science and DNA. For years, though, my true identity was hidden from me, buried beneath lies and falsehoods. I was fed a version of my life that wasn't true, and my real story was purposefully withheld. It wasn't until much later that the pieces started to fall into place, and I finally began to understand who I really was.

How do I feel about all of this? Well, there's a mix of emotions. On one hand, I'm relieved to know the truth now because so much of my childhood suddenly makes sense. On the other hand, there's a sense of frustration and sadness. Why did it take so long for the truth to come out? Why was I kept in the dark for so many years? But despite those feelings, I believe one thing strongly: if you truly love someone, you owe them the unadulterated truth. No matter how hard or complicated that truth may be, it's better than living in a world of deception.

My biological dad, Barack Obama Jr., did just that—he told me the truth. I know it sounds shocking to most, but he is my father. The moment of truth came in or about 1996, when I was a high school student at Heights High School in Wichita, Kansas. My guardians at the time gave me a heads-up that I'd be receiving a visit from a man who wanted to take me out of my current home. I had been lied to so many times about my family that I didn't know what to believe anymore. I had been told different men were my dad, so when my real dad showed up, I was skeptical.

When he arrived, he introduced himself and told me something that should have changed everything: "I'm your dad." Simple as that. But in my mind, I couldn't accept it. I was a traumatized teenager, and after hearing conflicting stories for years, I didn't know what to trust. My guardians had already planted seeds of doubt in my mind, telling me that this man wasn't my biological father. They said he was only pretending to be for financial gain or some other reason. At that point, I was done with all the stories. I wasn't ready to accept another version of reality, no matter how truthful it was.

Looking back on that day, I realize it wasn't just any ordinary visit. My father was preparing for something much bigger at the time—he was getting ready to run for the U.S. Senate. And as part of that process, he was dealing with the complexities of his personal life. There were reporters and news crews there at the high school, filming and documenting the moment. I remember the intense pressure I felt, but my behavior wasn't ideal for someone who was being filmed. I was anxious, confused, and frustrated, so I refused to be on camera or interviewed alongside him.

For anyone curious about this, you can find footage of him at Heights High School in Wichita, Kansas, in the second semester of 1996. It's out there in the archives for anyone interested in piecing together this part of history.

My interactions with my dad that day were complicated, to say the least. I wasn't just dealing with the overwhelming news that this man was my father, but I was also processing the pain of years of deceit. As he spoke to me, I remember him watching me closely. His expression was a mix of disbelief, shock, and something that I can now understand as hurt. He was my father, standing right in front of me, but I couldn't let myself believe it.

He brought his wife with him, and when he saw how I was responding—my tone, my body language, everything— he didn't push. He listened. But when I became disrespectful toward her, he stepped in. I'll never forget how he handled that moment. He told me in no uncertain terms, "You will not speak to her in that manner." It was the first time he spoke to me like a father—firm, protective, and demanding respect not just for himself but for his wife, too.

At the time, I couldn't see what was happening. I was too busy defending myself, thinking that I was the one being wronged. But in reality, I was doing a disservice to myself, to my future, and to the very bloodline that I should have been embracing. My response to him that day wasn't just out of teenage rebellion—it was rooted in years of trauma, confusion, and emotional wounds that hadn't healed.

The facts are there for anyone who cares to dig deeper. According to studies, childhood trauma, especially involving identity and family, can have long-lasting effects on a person's mental health. Research from the CDC shows that adverse childhood experiences (ACEs), like the kind I went through, can lead to higher risks of depression, anxiety, and even physical health problems later in life. For me, those feelings were very real and very much a part of how I reacted to my father in that moment.

But I now understand that I wasn't just hurting myself by rejecting him. I was rejecting the truth, the opportunity to know my real family, and the chance to build a relationship with my biological father—something that not everyone gets to do.

Growing up, I always had this nagging feeling that I didn't quite belong. I was raised by Tammie and Murphy Jr., who I was told were my biological parents, but deep down, something never felt right. It's hard to describe that kind of feeling as a child, but you just know when things don't add up. As a Taurus, loyalty runs deep in my blood. I naturally clung to the belief that the people raising me were telling the truth because why wouldn't they? But that loyalty also made it harder when I started to realize that the truth I had been told all my life might not be real.

I began asking questions. Who were my real parents? Why did I feel like an outsider in my own family? My hair, my skin, my features—they didn't quite match up with the family I was surrounded by. I wasn't treated like I was one of them, either. I was called names like "Peck-a-wood" and "Oreo," slurs that cut deep because they isolated me even more. I was too "white" for them, too "black" for others, always out of place, never quite fitting in. I wondered if this was what it felt like to be invisible, to not truly belong anywhere.

I wasn't just battling my identity but the treatment I received, too. I grew up in an environment where emotional, mental, and physical abuse became part of my daily life. The words hurt, but the actions cut deeper. For a long time, I built walls around myself—protective barriers to safeguard my mental health and my heart. It's what I had to do to survive. But even with all those defenses, I couldn't shake the need to know the truth about who I really was.

It wasn't until I grew older that everything started to unravel. I was born at St. Francis Hospital in Wichita, Kansas, on May 17, 1976—or so I thought. The reality was more complex than I could have ever imagined. My biological mother, Melinda Kay Atkins, had me during an illegal and unlawful adoption, changing my birth date to May 7, 1979. I had lived my entire life believing in a lie, and by the time I discovered the truth, both Melinda and Tammie were gone. They were dead, and so were the answers to all the questions I had bottled up inside me for years.

There's something unspeakably painful about losing your parents, no matter the circumstances. Studies show that the death of a parent is one of the most traumatic events anyone can go through. Psychologists have even found that children who lose a parent are at a higher risk of depression, anxiety, and long-term emotional distress. But the grief is compounded when you lose the very people who hold the answers to your identity. With both my adoptive and biological mothers gone, it felt like I had lost not just them but pieces of myself that I would never recover.

Tammie's death hit me hard. Despite everything—despite the abuse, the lies, the confusion—I still loved her. She had been diagnosed with a terminal illness, and watching her slowly succumb to it was heartbreaking. It's difficult to describe the emotions that flood you when you're sitting at the bedside of someone who raised you, knowing that every breath could be their last. I remember one of the last conversations we had. Tammie apologized to me—profusely, repeatedly. She said sorry for all the pain, all the hurt, all the things she had done to me. At the time, I didn't fully understand the weight of her words.

Then came the bombshell.

The last time I spoke with her, just before she passed away, she told me something that shook me to my core. She told me that my biological father was Barack Obama Jr. I remember the moment vividly—her lips moving slowly, barely able to speak, but the words were clear as day. "Barack Obama is your real dad," she said. I was in disbelief. How could that possibly be true? Was it the medication talking, the morphine clouding her mind? Or was she speaking her truth?

At that moment, all I could do was hold her, whispering prayers for her peaceful transition. I lay there in the hospital bed with her, hugging her, telling her I would always love her no matter what. It didn't matter that the truth was painful or confusing; it didn't matter that I would never fully understand what had happened. All I knew was that I forgave her. I had to, for my own peace of mind.

We buried her on President's Day in 2020. It's strange to think about it now—how symbolic it felt. My adoptive mother, Tammie, always lived a life of secrets and struggles, and when she passed, I knew her funeral on President's Day wasn't just a coincidence. It was deliberate. My adoptive family used that day to bury more than just her body. They wanted to bury the truth about my biological father. My aunt and sister even mentioned it to me, saying, "Lata, it's ironic that Tammie is being buried on President's Day."

At the time, I thought it was just another offhand comment from her, but deep down, I knew there was more to it. I had heard the story before—on multiple occasions—about who my real dad was. Tammie wasn't one to keep her thoughts to herself, especially when it came to big secrets. But she had her demons, too, and most people around her didn't take her words seriously.

Tammie had battled addiction most of her life. She always claimed it wasn't her fault. "I was drugged," she used to tell me, "forced to take them so I wouldn't reveal the truth to you." She swore she had been silenced, a victim of a bigger conspiracy. As much as I wanted to believe her, it was hard. She was in and out of treatment centers, hospitals, and, at one point, even mental institutions. But her words lingered. They always did.

The first time I heard the truth, it didn't really sink in. I was sitting in the house where I grew up, just an ordinary day, watching TV. My uncle, who had been around for most of my childhood, suddenly looked at my mom and said, "Tammie, are you going to tell her?" She looked me dead in the eye and said, "So, uh, Lata, that's your real dad." I glanced at the screen. The man she was pointing at was none other than Barack Obama. Yes, *that* Barack Obama.

I laughed it off. It seemed too wild, too far-fetched to even be true. Barack Obama, a man who was making headlines across the world, running for President of the United States, was my biological father? No way. It felt like one of those made-for-TV moments. I shook my head and said a quick prayer for the man's safety. At that time, I didn't believe a word of what she said, but I was worried that such a huge lie could be dangerous for him.

It wasn't until later that I began to piece together fragments of memories. I had forgotten about the time he visited my school in 1996. I eventually recalled his presence at my first wedding in 1999 in the Mosque in Wichita, Kansas. I realized I had blocked out so many moments, most likely due to the PTSD I carried from years of childhood trauma.

Growing up, life wasn't easy. I endured more than any child should—physical, emotional, and mental abuse, neglect, and even human trafficking. I still remember the time when I was hit so hard that it detached the retina in my eye. It took years for me to process all the trauma, and during that time, I built walls around myself, locking away memories that hurt too much to confront. So, when my mother confessed that Obama was my biological father, I just laughed. I wasn't ready to accept it. Not then.

But the truth has a funny way of creeping up on you, no matter how deeply you try to bury it.

On May 7, 2019, my birthday, everything changed. It was the last time I would ever hear my mother's voice wishing me a happy birthday. Tammie was in her final days, diagnosed with stage four colon cancer. She called me, her voice fragile and weak, but her humor still intact. "So, uh, happy birthday, daughter!" she said, laughing at her own joke. We both burst out laughing, knowing that it would probably be the last time we'd share such a moment.

As much as we laughed, there was a deep sadness in her voice that I couldn't ignore. She told me, "I won't be here next year, but I want you to know that I love you. I'm sorry for everything I put you through." I assured her that I loved her too and that all the hardships had only made me stronger. "If anyone wants to see me fold, they'll have to catch me at the laundromat!" I joked, trying to lighten the mood.

But the weight of her words lingered. She had been both a mother and a sister to me, given how close we were in age.

We grew up together, surviving the chaos of life side by side. As much as I loved her, I couldn't forget the pain and suffering I had endured. But that day, as she apologized, I felt her sorrow and her need for redemption. I wanted her to find peace, both in this world and the next.

Her passing on February 7, 2020, felt like the end of an era. The finality of it was overwhelming. And as the years passed, I began to understand that her secret—the one about my father—wasn't just a figment of her imagination. It was real. Barack Obama was my father.

The years following her death were a whirlwind. I spent my time digging through old memories, connecting the dots, and trying to come to terms with my new reality. In many ways, the revelation didn't change who I was. I had already survived the worst that life could throw at me. But it gave me a sense of clarity, a missing piece of the puzzle that had always been there, hidden just beneath the surface.

Chapter 2: The Name and Its Significance

Names are powerful. They shape how people see us, sometimes even how we see ourselves. My name is Lata Leare. That's what my biological father, Barack, named me. I've learned it's a beautiful, resilient Indian name. "Lata" means "creeper" or "vine" in Sanskrit—a name often given to girls born in the spring. And there's a special kind of meaning behind it. Creeper vines are known to grow no matter what, pushing through the soil and climbing toward the light, even in the toughest conditions. It's a reminder of resilience, of growth, and, oddly enough, of bravery.

Growing up, I learned that in Hindu culture, names often carry deep symbolic meanings. For instance, the name "Lata" is thought to hold the spirit of resilience, representing someone who can bend without breaking, survive storms, and keep growing even when things get rough. This meaning resonated with me on many levels. Resilience and courage are two qualities that have shaped my journey in ways I never imagined.

Names like Lata aren't uncommon in India. One of the most famous women with my name was Lata Mangeshkar, an extraordinary singer who earned the title "Queen of Melody." Her songs have been part of Indian culture for generations, filling homes, festivals, and celebrations with music. There's also Lata Thakur, a politician who worked hard to improve the lives of people in her community, and Lata Mondal, a cricketer from Bangladesh, who's also known for her strength and perseverance. I couldn't help but wonder if these strong women had a bit of that resilient "vine" spirit, too.

The funny part, though, is that even though "Lata" was my real name, the people who raised me insisted that it was spelled "Lata" but pronounced "Yetta." It felt strange, like wearing a shoe that didn't quite fit. Somehow, I think they wanted to erase parts of me without outright changing my name. Instead of Lata Leare, they changed my middle name to Leah, and my last name became Tomlinson. It was like my identity was wrapped up and hidden in some way that even I couldn't fully understand for years.

Then there's my middle name, Leare, which is even more mysterious. Unlike "Lata," I haven't found many people with this name, but I learned that Leare might mean "love canoe goddess" in Hawaiian culture. I've wondered if my father chose that because he wanted me to remember something important about my family history, something that could stand as a reminder of where I came from.

But then, as I uncovered more of my story, I realized there might be an even deeper reason behind the name. There were whispers of a connection to the Queen of England, like a mysterious link I was never supposed to discover. It's strange to think that my name could hold such a heavy story, a tale that spanned continents and cultures, from the Hawaiian seas to the royal halls of England.

When my name changed from Lata Leare Obama to Lata Leare Tomlinson, it wasn't just a change of letters on paper. It felt like they were erasing pieces of me, replacing parts of my story with one that wasn't mine. Imagine one day being told that your name is spelled differently or pronounced another way and being told that it's better this way or that it's "just the way it is." It's like telling a story over and over until you don't recognize it anymore.

This change wasn't limited to just my name. My entire identity, even my date of birth, was altered. It was like I was given a whole new story, and I had to live within it, even though something inside me knew it didn't quite fit. Every child has a right to know where they come from and who they are, but that right was taken from me in a calculated way.

The truth can sometimes be like pieces of a puzzle, hidden away in different places. For me, some of those pieces were in sealed court records, hidden family pictures, and even hospital records. It's strange to think that official documents could contain pieces of my story I had never seen. But there they were, all sealed away, as if hiding those pieces would hide my real self. When I began learning these details, it felt like the world started to make more sense.

Finding the truth wasn't easy. It meant going through records, asking questions, and sometimes facing answers that were hard to hear. But each piece of information helped me understand who I was meant to be. I think many people, even those who don't have the exact experiences I've had, can relate to this search for identity. We all want to understand where we come from and what makes us who we are.

The false family that raised me didn't just give me a different middle name; they told me the meaning of that name. Leah, as they explained, is from the Bible. Leah appears in the Old Testament, in the book of Genesis. Her story is one of endurance, and some say her name means "weary." The word "weary" certainly resonates with me. Sometimes, the search for truth is exhausting. It's wearying to dig and search, especially when you're going against everything you've been told.

But Leah's story wasn't just about being weary; it was about strength, persistence, and resilience, even when times were tough. In a way, I could see pieces of myself in her story, too. She may have felt weary, but she was still part of an important journey, a greater story that kept moving forward. Much like Leah, I was given a role in a story that I didn't choose but one that I had to carry through with courage and grace.

Looking back, I think my father named me Lata Leare for a reason. The vine, or creeper plant, isn't always beautiful or celebrated, but it's strong and resilient. It weaves through rocks, climbs over obstacles, and reaches for the sun no matter what. It grows in unexpected places and adapts, finding its way through challenges that seem insurmountable. That's what I've had to do, too.

Being resilient doesn't mean that everything is easy or that things don't hurt. It means you find a way through, no matter how hard it gets. And maybe, just maybe, my name was meant to remind me of that strength. Even when others tried to change who I was or hide pieces of my past, I was still Lata. The name was there like a hidden root, growing beneath the surface.

Every day, I discover more pieces of who I am, and I grow stronger. I'm learning to embrace the name Lata, a name of resilience, and Leare, a name that holds stories I'm still uncovering. Though there are still questions and mysteries, I hold onto the fact that my name is a part of me that no one can take away.

My journey is far from over, but I'm proud of how far I've come. For every person who has ever felt like they didn't quite belong like they were living someone else's story, I hope my story offers a little bit of hope. Our names, our identities, and our pasts are ours to claim, even if we have to search for them. We're all vines growing toward the sun, no matter the obstacles in our path.

Chapter 3: Early Childhood Memories

From the moment we're born, we start piecing together the story of who we are. As babies, we don't know a thing about family trees or where we came from, but we know the faces and voices of the people who love us. We know hugs, warm meals, and safe arms around us. And as we grow, we learn little things about ourselves—our likes, dislikes, habits, and quirks. For most people, those pieces build up over time to form a clear picture. But for me, discovering who I really am has been a journey full of twists, turns, and surprising revelations. My name is Lata Leare Obama, and this is my story.

I was born in Wichita, Kansas, but my story begins with two very young parents who had no idea how complicated things were about to become. You see, my biological parents were underage, which meant they couldn't legally take care of me in the ways most parents can. So, my path was immediately different from other kids. My early childhood became a story of secrets, questions, and, eventually, resilience.

From a young age, I was told that my adoptive family, the Tomlinsons, was my real family. I grew up believing that Tammie D. Tomlinson was my birth mother and that Murphy B. Atkins Jr. was my birth father. Those names felt so solid, so permanent—like the foundation on which my life was built. I couldn't have known then that this foundation was shaky, full of falsehoods and misunderstandings.

As I grew older, however, I started questioning things, little details that didn't add up. It was in the late 90s when my curiosity led me on a search for answers. I wanted to understand more about who I was and where I came from, so I went to Seattle, Washington, hoping to connect with people who could fill in the blanks. This is where things took a turn I never expected. A woman, Melinda K. Atkins, who I initially thought was my aunt, told me something that sent my world spinning: she claimed she was my birth mother.

Can you imagine hearing something like that after believing a completely different story your entire life? I was shocked, hurt, and confused. Every memory I had suddenly felt fragile, like it could shatter at any moment. I called Tammie and Zelma Tomlinson to ask them about what I had heard, hoping they'd clear things up, but they denied it all. They insisted that Tammie and Murphy were my biological parents, dismissing what Melinda had told me.

Over time, though, I would come to find that what Melinda had told me was true. Not only was she my birth mother, but my father was none other than Barack Obama Jr., a name known around the world, a name that carries immense weight. To say that this revelation changed my life is an understatement. It was like discovering I had a whole other life that had been hidden from me, a legacy I'd never been allowed to explore.

For years, my adoptive family went to great lengths to keep me in the dark about who I truly was. Looking back now, I understand that they must have had their reasons, but those reasons hurt me deeply. By keeping me away from my biological parents and extended family, they took away the chance for me to form those early, foundational bonds. Bonds that experts say shape the person you become in ways you can't always see but are always there, like a guiding force in the background. Studies show that children who have strong connections to their family and cultural history tend to be more resilient and confident. I wonder sometimes if my life would have been different, simpler, maybe if I'd had that foundation from the start.

This lack of family connection wasn't the only thing that hurt me. Over the years, the Tomlinsons took things from me that went far beyond my sense of identity. From financial assets to property, they stole from me repeatedly. They even found ways to control and manipulate law enforcement to keep me from reporting these thefts. Imagine the helplessness of knowing something is rightfully yours yet having no power to defend it. I wasn't only robbed of my possessions but also of my peace of mind and safety.

One of the most devastating losses was my lottery winnings. I'd been fortunate enough to hold a winning ticket, only to have it stolen and cashed without my consent. The law is supposed to protect people, especially victims of theft, but in my case, my adoptive family and even a former partner went to extreme measures to prevent me from getting justice. Bribing law enforcement officers, falsifying documents—these actions were like bricks in a wall meant to keep me from my own life.

Another painful part of my journey has been the theft of my creative work. You might've heard of a book called *Pimpology: The 48 Laws of the Game*. I wrote that, but I've seen royalties go to people who had nothing to do with its creation. If you've ever poured your heart into something—a painting, a story, a piece of music—you know how much of yourself is embedded in that work. To have that taken from you feels like someone has reached inside and stolen a piece of your soul.

Despite all this, I have a fierce determination to stand tall, to find my voice, and to share my story. I want people to understand that I'm not just the "daughter of a former president" or a "victim of a fraudulent family." I'm someone who fought to reclaim her identity, to understand her roots, and to connect with the family that was hidden from her. Every day, I get a little closer to healing, reclaiming what was taken, and being proud of who I am and where I come from.

Barack Obama once said, "The best way to not feel hopeless is to get up and do something." These words resonate deeply with me. It took years, but I eventually found my strength and my voice, and I'm learning to stand up for myself. My story may have started in secrecy and confusion, but I'm determined that it won't end there.

When I think back on the life I've lived, I realize just how many battles I've faced. My civil rights were violated repeatedly, my voice drowned out in a sea of control and manipulation, and my choices were taken from me before I even knew I had them. Imagine having decisions about your health, your body, and your life taken out of your hands entirely—being treated as if you had no say, no rights. That was my reality, shaped by people who should have protected me but instead used me for their gain.

In a world that prides itself on freedom and individual rights, my life felt like a contradiction. I was forced into situations that no one should ever endure, and my boundaries were ignored time and time again. Medical procedures were performed on me without my consent, and I was put into government experiments against my will, experiences that were terrifying, isolating, and sometimes even painful. These were things I didn't understand at the time—how could I? I was young, unprepared, and had no control over what was happening.

I remember every moment of it, the times I felt like a test subject rather than a person, and the trauma has stayed with me to this day. The people who were supposed to care for me, who should have had my best interests at heart, betrayed me on a level that's hard to put into words. My adoptive family, in particular, was at the heart of this deception. They orchestrated and supported the lies, creating a twisted web of control that kept me in their grasp for far too long. I know this isn't something people like to hear; it's uncomfortable to think about family in that way. But the truth is that not everyone is meant to protect you—sometimes, they're the ones who pose the greatest threat.

In my heart, I knew something was missing, a part of me that I couldn't quite put my finger on. Even as a young child, I felt this inexplicable pull, a desire for connection and understanding that went unanswered. I'd spend nights imagining my real family, the people who shared my blood and my history, and I wondered if they were looking for me, too.

The truth, as I came to discover, was as unexpected as it was painful. My biological father, Barack Obama Jr., was someone I'd admired from afar, never realizing he was so much closer to me than I'd ever known. As the former president of the United States, he stood as a symbol of resilience, intelligence, and courage. And here I was, his daughter, navigating a life so removed from his own that it seemed surreal.

But the memories I have of him, the real ones, are comforting in their simplicity. When I was small, he taught me to be fearless. I was scared of the toy Jack-in-the-Box, and he'd sit with me, helping me face my fear of the unknown. "Expect the unexpected," he'd say, smiling with that calm, reassuring warmth that only a father can give. Those words have stayed with me, even in the toughest times, and they've been my guiding light through the darkest moments.

The legal side of things is a nightmare to navigate. Imagine sealed court documents and secret files holding the answers to the injustice I endured. Statistics show that even today, about 1 in 3 women experience abuse at the hands of someone they know, but so few of these cases make it to court. So many people suffer in silence, their stories unheard, and I often wonder if things would be different if more people had the courage to speak out. I know my story is just one among many, but it's my hope that sharing it might inspire others to stand up for themselves, reclaim their rights, and seek justice.

Through it all, I held onto the hope that one day, the truth would come to light. That justice, elusive as it may seem, would prevail. The people who facilitated the abuse, who controlled and manipulated my life, would finally be held accountable. I pray every day that an investigation will be opened to uncover the depths of this wrongdoing and bring these individuals to justice. It's not just about me; it's about a broken system that allows abuse to go unchecked and unpunished.

I know it sounds intense, but think about it: each year, thousands of children and adults alike are subjected to situations where their rights are overlooked or flat-out ignored. They don't have a voice, or if they do, it's not strong enough to break through the noise. But I've learned that persistence is key, and every person has the power to make a difference, even if it feels like the odds are stacked against them.

To my father, Barack, or "*Abu*," as I sometimes call him in my heart, I want you to know that I'm here, waiting, hoping for a chance to connect with you. Life separated us for reasons I can't fully understand, but that bond, that connection, is something I feel every day. You taught me so much without even knowing it—strength, courage, and the importance of staying true to myself. I want you to know that I'm ready to build a relationship with you, to fill in the gaps that have left me feeling so incomplete.

Family is supposed to be our first source of love, safety, and support. I missed out on that, but I'm ready to reclaim it. So, if you're out there reading this, please know that your daughter is waiting, eager to reconnect and rebuild what was lost.

I've spent too long being afraid, too long letting others dictate my story. It's time to reclaim my voice, to take back what was taken from me, and forge a path forward. This isn't just about justice—it's about healing, about finding closure and creating a new life on my own terms.

In this chapter of my life, I'm determined to rewrite the narrative, to bring the truth to light, and stand up for myself in a way I never could before. And for anyone reading this, I want you to know that there's always hope, even in the darkest moments. Statistics might suggest that people in situations like mine rarely find justice, but I believe in the power of persistence in the resilience of the human spirit. And I believe, above all, that it's never too late to seek the life we deserve.

I'm sharing this story not just for myself but for anyone who has ever felt powerless, anyone who's had their rights stripped away or their voice silenced. There's strength in numbers, and together, we can demand a system that values justice, truth, and compassion.

Chapter 4: The Lies I Was Told

Growing up, I always felt like an outsider, even in my own family. I didn't fit the mold that surrounded me; my words, my manners, and my values seemed to set me apart in ways that became clear at an early age. I remember reading *Dick and Jane* books and comics in the newspaper while my family watched TV. While the characters in those stories lived in worlds that seemed orderly and logical, I lived in a world of contrasts and hidden truths.

My love for reading only deepened this feeling of difference. As I read, I noticed how words were supposed to sound. So, when I'd hear my family say "skreet" instead of "street," I couldn't help but correct them. I was just trying to help, but they didn't see it that way. Instead, they would accuse me of trying to "act white" or of "talking like a white girl." This puzzled me, especially since I had caramel-colored skin like everyone else in my family. It made me wonder why they saw my behavior as so different and where I fit into this family dynamic. I didn't yet understand that my mixed heritage—the part of me that came from my biological father—had an impact on how they saw me and, ultimately, how they treated me.

In whispers and passing comments, I would overhear things about my granny taking care of us "to keep the money going." I didn't know it then, but these whispers hinted that my biological dad had a role in supporting me financially, even if I was oblivious to it. To others, I looked different from my adoptive sisters, and people would often ask why I didn't resemble either of them or my adoptive mother, Tammie. I wasn't privy to the family's secrets and could only feel the weight of not fully belonging. There was this odd story about my arrival, too: my family claimed I had been delivered by a stork. I knew storks didn't bring babies. But back then, that story felt like a game—a part of the world I didn't fully understand.

Everything changed one day when I was visiting family in Washington. I met Melinda, a woman whose face mirrored mine in unexpected ways. It was more than a resemblance; it felt like looking at a missing part of myself. Then, Melinda took my hand, looked into my eyes, and told me something that would change my life forever: "I'm your birth mother."

At that moment, questions flooded my mind. Could this be true? Why would the Tomlinsons, the family I'd known and trusted, hide such a life-changing truth from me? But there was a gentleness in Melinda's eyes, a look of shared pain and unspoken history. Her words carried weight, yet they seemed impossible. When I returned to my adoptive family for answers, they denied Melinda's claim, leaving me stranded in a sea of confusion and frustration.

Living in a world where I wasn't told the truth about myself left scars. The Tomlinsons' deception went beyond simple lies; it undermined my ability to understand who I was. Growing up with these half-truths and outright lies shaped my confidence, my trust in others, and, most painfully, my sense of self. I constantly felt like an outsider, not only in the world at large but in my own family. I was left wondering who I could have been if only I had known where I came from.

One of the hardest parts of this journey was realizing how much time had been stolen from me. The time that I could have spent bonding with my biological father, who, as I would eventually learn, shared my love for knowledge and learning. Imagine the guidance I could have had, the help with homework, the deeper conversations about books and ideas, and the encouragement to dream big. My whole life, I had this unexplainable drive to attend Harvard. Now, I know why. It's in my DNA; it was a dream my father might have had for himself and, perhaps, for me, too.

Time is one of those things you can never get back. Losing that precious time due to the choices of others is a hurt that doesn't easily fade. Statistically, around 135,000 children are adopted every year in the United States, many growing up without knowing their biological parents or their full histories. Some find out their stories, while others are left with unanswered questions. I was one of those kids, navigating an identity built on half-truths.

Despite the confusion and hardship, I held onto my dreams. As an adult, I even ran for a seat in the Kansas State House of Representatives, District 89. I wanted to make a difference, to represent people like me who might feel overlooked or underestimated. But the campaign process was challenging, and I couldn't help but think about how much a father's guidance could have strengthened my confidence. His words, his wisdom—both were absent, leaving me to navigate on my own.

Running for office without his backing made me realize how deeply those family secrets had impacted my journey. Imagine this: if I had grown up knowing who I was and where I came from, maybe I would have been more grounded and more confident. Maybe I would have had a better shot at securing that seat and influencing my community in meaningful ways.

This journey taught me that life doesn't always unfold as planned. It taught me that family is complex and that sometimes, those closest to us keep secrets to protect themselves rather than to protect us. But through all the hurt, the identity struggles, and the searching, I have also learned resilience. I may have lost time, but I won't let it define the rest of my life.

Every journey for justice has its own soundtrack, and for me, that anthem is Bob Marley's *Get Up, Stand Up*. Every time I hear "stand up for your rights," it feels like a rallying cry, a reminder that my fight isn't just personal but also universal. My life has been a path of pushing back against the injustices I've faced, one step at a time, and with every challenge, those lyrics replay in my head, giving me the fuel I need to keep moving forward.

Another phrase that resonates deeply with me is "No justice, no peace." It's as if these words connect me with all the others who've stood up against the odds, people who've refused to accept an unfair world as it is. Justice isn't just a goal for me; it's an unbreakable part of my journey. I've learned that pursuing it means facing down my fears, speaking up, and sometimes standing alone, as many before me have done. Legends like Muhammad Ali come to mind. He wasn't just a fighter in the ring; he was a champion for equality and change, facing battles beyond boxing for a cause larger than himself.

Like Ali, I've had to train for my own battles. The hard knocks I took growing up were painful, but each one taught me something new. Every time I felt like I didn't belong or faced an obstacle, it was like a round in the ring, pushing me to become more resilient. I may not win every round, and I certainly haven't so far, but the winner is the one who's still standing at the end. That's what drives me—to keep getting up, no matter how hard the hits.

My father's words, "Fired up, ready to go," echo in my heart and mind. I carry that phrase with me as a reminder that my journey is just getting started. His words are a part of me now, a motivation that runs as deep as my dreams. And while I may not know the outcome, I know I'm still here, still standing, still fighting.

In the end, I'm a fighter, and my fight is far from over. Standing up for my rights, seeking justice, and honoring my story is what makes me feel alive. I may not win every battle, but I am in this for the long haul.

Chapter 5: Abuse, Survival, and Strength

The world was simple when I was a child, or at least I thought it was. I believed adults were there to protect us, to make things safe and warm. It's strange how we're born trusting, clinging to a world we think won't hurt us. Looking back, I wish someone had told me that sometimes, the people we're supposed to trust the most are the ones who do the deepest harm.

My innocence was taken from me when I was barely old enough to understand what innocence was. I was a preschooler, spending my days in laughter and play and my nights in the warm comfort of family, or so I thought. My adoptive mother, Tammie, often left me with her brother, my uncle, when she wanted to go out. It was just a normal part of life: she would head to the club, and I'd stay with him in the townhouse basement, where he lived.

One night, things took a darker turn. My uncle started the evening by letting me ride my little bike around the basement and play hide-and-seek. His laughs, his voice—everything about it felt like another game. But eventually, the games slowed down, and I got sleepy. I lay on the bed, my small body curled up, trusting that I was safe. I was just a child, blissfully unaware of the danger lying right beside me.

When I awoke, it was an experience that would leave permanent scars on my soul. I opened my eyes to something cold and painful: hands that didn't feel like they belonged, touches that stung like fire. It was a pain that tore through me, leaving me breathless, my screams echoing off the empty walls. Blood was everywhere. I must have passed out several times because I remember only patches of it—flashes of pain, his face, and then darkness. I yelled, I screamed, but no one came. It was just me and him in that basement, alone with a secret I was too young to understand.

When Tammie came back that night, she found me sobbing in a corner, still in pain. She didn't say much, didn't look me in the eye. Instead, she took me straight to her mother's house, where anger and tears filled the air. I remember Tammie pacing and muttering to herself, her face twisted in anger as she repeated, "My brother. My own brother." They called my Aunt Sherry, who came over to help. She put me in a bath, scrubbing the blood from my skin, her hands gentle but distant. I winced, telling her how much it hurt, but she just kept washing, her eyes hollow, not daring to look at me directly.

After that night, something shifted. Tammie looked at me differently, almost like I was a reminder of something she wanted to forget. Soon enough, she sat me down, her face wet with tears, pleading with me to keep quiet. She warned me about the consequences if I spoke out, saying both she and her brother would go to jail if anyone knew the truth. She begged and sobbed, making me feel as if I held the power to destroy everything. I was so young, too young to understand, but I knew how to obey. And I did—out of love, out of fear, or maybe just out of survival.

Not everyone wanted me to stay silent. My grandmother, Grandma Toot, always told me to be truthful. "The truth will set you free, darling," she would say, her words full of hope and promise. She said that telling the truth would give me a better life and a brighter future. But I was too small to see it her way. All I could see was Tammie's desperation, her begging me not to talk, her fear of prison. So, when they questioned me at school, I said nothing. I kept my head down and my mouth shut, hiding everything inside.

Growing up, violence was a shadow that followed me. My stepfather, Paul, was another source of pain. He was rough and cold, his hands heavy, his words sharper than any weapon. One day, he kicked me in the face so hard it detached the retina in my right eye. That same day, he stomped on Tammie's head, leaving bruises and cuts, his boots making sickening sounds against her skull. The violence was just another part of life. Bruises healed, cuts scarred, but we endured.

Paul's abuse eventually went too far, and Tammie reached her breaking point. I was with her the day she decided enough was enough. It was April 15, 1985, a day I'll never forget. She stood there, gun in hand, her body trembling but determined. I watched as she emptied all six shots of her .22-caliber revolver into his upper body, putting an end to years of pain and fear. Later, the state of Kansas would acquit her because of something called Battered

Woman Syndrome. She became the first Black woman in Kansas to be acquitted on such grounds. People talk about it as a landmark case, but for me, it was just another scar, another piece of a broken childhood.

Life taught me early on that silence was survival. Speaking out was dangerous, a threat to the fragile web of lies holding us together. Each time I tried to share my pain, my words were twisted, brushed off as "bad dreams" or "evil spirits." My family dismissed my voice, telling me to forget, to pretend, to bury it all. And so, for years, I did. But silence didn't save me; it only locked me in a cage.

I learned to protect myself. My uncle, ironically, had been the one to teach me how to handle a gun. He'd taken Tammie and me to the park, where he showed us how to aim, shoot, and hit our targets without fail. "Headshots are best," he'd say, his voice calm, his hand guiding mine. His training became my survival. I was a young girl learning skills meant for protection, taught by the very person who'd shattered my world.

As I grew older, the abuse didn't stop, but my reaction to it did. Men in my family, people I was supposed to trust, treated me like their secret, their possession. But eventually, I stopped being silent. When someone threatened me, I'd look them straight in the eyes and say, "Do you think the good Lord stopped making killers when he made you?" I was done being a victim. My voice was my weapon, my shield, my freedom. They must have seen the fire in my eyes because the abuse eventually ceased. They still looked, they still whispered, but they no longer dared to touch.

I discovered the magic of words when I was very young. Stories became my haven, pages my refuge, and each book I opened was a doorway into a world far removed from my own. Reading allowed me to escape the turmoil surrounding me, filling my mind with the kind of peace I could rarely find elsewhere. By losing myself in books, I found a path to my dreams, a vision of what my life could be beyond survival. Somewhere between the lines, I started to dream of college, of one day becoming a lawyer, a voice for those who needed it most.

The odds were always stacked against me. "You'll be lucky if you even finish high school," they'd say, dismissing my ambitions as if I were foolish for dreaming them. It's strange how those words of doubt pushed me harder, making me even more determined to succeed. With every book I read and every story I absorbed, I became more certain that I could achieve what they said I couldn't. Education became my armor, a layer of resilience built one page, one lesson at a time.

When I entered high school, I threw myself into my studies, working harder than anyone else, often staying up late into the night, determined to rise above the doubts that had been planted around me. My drive paid off, and soon, I found myself in honors classes, pushing my limits academically and earning my place among the best students. By the time I reached my senior year, I was already taking college courses. It was a small step toward my dream, but each class and each credit earned felt like a victory.

I went on to earn my associate's degree from Butler County Community College in El Dorado, Kansas. The joy I felt walking across that stage was something no one could take from me—it was my first taste of freedom, of breaking free from the chains of doubt and limitations that others had set for me. But I didn't stop there. I knew I had more in me, so I kept going, enrolling at Wichita State University and earning my bachelor's degree. I kept my gaze steady on the path ahead, my ambitions urging me forward.

Education became my escape, my solace, and my purpose. After Wichita State, I pursued a master's degree at Baker University, the oldest university in Kansas, knowing that each step I took would bring me closer to my goal. My dreams of becoming a lawyer still called to me, their whispers growing louder with every achievement. And even though life sometimes threw me off course—like the time my tuition was stolen, halting my pursuit of a Doctorate in Business Administration—I never stopped dreaming. The setbacks were just another part of the journey.

Through all of this, books were my constant companions. They filled my world with knowledge and ideas, allowing me to mentally escape the confines of my reality. Reading wasn't just a hobby; it was a lifeline. Stories of survival, resilience, and redemption resonated with me deeply, reminding me that others, too, had walked through the fire and come out on the other side.

Maya Angelou's writing, especially, became a guiding light, her words capturing so much of the pain, resilience, and strength that I felt. Like her, I had once been silenced by my experiences, but through reading her work, I found the courage to find my own voice again. Her words taught me the power of self-forgiveness, that healing begins when we forgive ourselves, realizing that the past was not our fault. I was also subjected to MK Ultra. My false family placed me in this program, where I endured gang-stalking, being "doppelgänged," experimentation, and even forced participation in a breeding program, among other traumas. I am now speaking my truth in the hope that justice will be served and I will receive compensation for these acts committed against me without my knowledge or consent.

In addition to my previously mentioned educational accomplishments, I am also a certified paralegal, having earned my certification from the Emory Continuing Education Center in Atlanta, GA.

I often think of myself as a lotus, a flower that blooms through mud, rising resilient and beautiful from the darkest depths. The trials, the struggles, and every tear I shed were just the mud, shaping me, nourishing the roots of my determination. I am here today because I never let go of that vision of who I could become. My tenacity to survive, to rise, and to keep moving forward became my greatest strength. And I know Allah has been with me through every step, guiding me, lifting me when I felt like falling, and reminding me that I am not alone in this journey. Every night spent with tear-stained pillows was a night I chose to swim, to stay afloat rather than drown in my sorrow.

Looking back, I realize that my journey was a gradual climb, a hard-fought path of resilience. There were moments of doubt, nights when I felt like I was carrying the weight of the world alone. But those moments didn't break me; they only sharpened my determination. I crowned myself long before anyone else could, embracing my worth and standing tall in the face of my trials. My journey wasn't easy, and the crown I wear today is one I've earned through resilience, hard work, and an unshakable belief in my own strength.

Now, I am ready to speak my truth and let my voice be heard. I am here, standing in my own power, looking ahead to the dreams that have yet to be fulfilled. The girl who was once told she would never graduate high school has earned her degrees and built a future she could once only imagine. I am here, a testament to the power of perseverance, proof that with enough determination and faith, you can rise from any circumstance.

And so, as I continue this journey, I know that each step forward is a celebration, a reminder that I am not defined by what happened to me but by what I chose to become. This crown of resilience is mine, and I wear it proudly, knowing that I have the strength to overcome anything life brings my way.

Chapter 6: The Encounter at Heights High School

The day my father came to visit wasn't intense or explosive like I imagined it might be. No, it was calm, surreal, almost like a scene from a movie—except I was right there in it. I didn't know then how much that day would mean to me, how much of the truth I was hearing for the first time. My adoptive family had coached me well, filling my head with stories about how he only wanted to claim me to get his hands on the money they said was his real interest. According to them, he didn't care about me at all.

But the truth was far more complicated than the simple story they'd spun. Standing before me, in all his calm confidence, was my biological father. He was soft-spoken, kind, and gentle yet assertive as he spoke. "I'm your dad," he told me, and there was no room for questioning it. He wasn't here for some twisted game of wealth or power—he was here to tell me the truth.

He had sent carnations—red, pink, and white—days before, each one a little hint of what he felt. The note had been simple: *Love, Dad.* At the time, I didn't want to believe it. But now, standing there in the same room with him, everything began to unravel. This man was here for me, not because of the lies they'd filled my head with.

There he stood, as I'd later come to realize, with the same steady demeanor he held on television. It was calm but filled with purpose, a quiet kind of strength. He was like that song, *Smooth Operator* by Sade, which he'd sometimes hum when he visited. As I listened to him, I wanted to give in, to let myself believe everything he was saying. But the hurt I carried from years of lies and betrayal sat deep within me, like a wall I couldn't break down just yet.

The truth was, I'd always felt a little different, like I didn't belong. My adoptive family hadn't exactly filled my life with love and reassurance. Instead, I often felt I was on a battlefield—alone. They'd lied to me so many times that, even now, when the truth was right in front of me, I couldn't fully accept it. My father, sensing this, didn't push. He listened to every word I had to say and then told me that he would respect my wishes. I saw in his eyes that he wished things could be different, but he wasn't going to force it.

My father's calm confidence, his sense of purpose, and his gentle demeanor—all stayed with me even as he left that day. He had attended my conference, learned about my grades, and even complimented me for being in honors classes. I had always wondered why the news cameras were around that day. It turned out they weren't there by coincidence. They had come to capture this meeting, to record the story of him reaching out to his biological daughter. He was running for political office at the time, but his commitment to me was just as clear.

I remember the reporters' reactions, the mix of surprise and anticipation in the room as they watched us. But at that moment, I didn't care about the cameras. My heart was overwhelmed, filled with emotions I couldn't quite understand. My adoptive family had said he was only here for himself, for his career, or for his money. But it was obvious to me now that this man, my father, had come because he wanted to be here for me.

One memory from that day still brings a smile to my face. My father loved to dance, and it was one thing even my adoptive family mentioned—my dad could really dance. We'd listen to *He's the Greatest Dancer* by Sister Sledge, and he'd show me the steps. I remember standing on top of his feet as he glided across the floor, teaching me how to follow the rhythm. Those moments were brief but unforgettable, giving me a rare glimpse of what life could have been like with him there all along.

Dancing with him felt like one of the few real connections we could have beyond the words and the walls I'd built. For a few minutes, I could let go of my doubts and just be present with him, trusting that he had always wanted the best for me.

Unfortunately, the visit wasn't as sweet when my adoptive family got involved. They hadn't been excited to see him there; instead, they questioned why he'd come after all this time. They threw in their own jabs, dismissing him, reminding me of all the supposed "abandonment." The truth was, they had been benefiting financially, and if my father had gained access to me, they risked losing that. They didn't care about what was best for me. They saw me as an asset, a paycheck they didn't want to lose.

The reality sank in even deeper when I thought back to the house on North Holyoke in Wichita, Kansas—the very one my father had helped them buy. That home had been left to me by my adoptive grandfather, yet it was taken and sold without my consent, along with land in Tomlinson Hill, Texas. Assets meant for me had been stolen, swept up in their web of deceit. It was another betrayal, one that I would only fully understand years later.

It took me a long time to process that day, to understand that my father had done his part, financially and emotionally, even if I hadn't been ready to receive it. Back then, the wounds were too fresh, the trust too broken. But now, with years behind me and clarity before me, I can see everything that he tried to offer. I know that someday we'll have the reunion I'd once been too scared to believe in. When that day comes, I'll be ready to embrace him fully, to dance with him again, just like we did all those years ago.

Looking back, I see how much that moment shaped the person I've become. It was a turning point, though I didn't realize it at the time, a chance for me to look at the truth in the face, to see my father for who he really was. But back then, I was too young, too guarded to understand it. His calmness and sincerity were gifts, ones I couldn't fully accept. As a parent myself now, I look back and understand that he did what was best. He came to me with honesty, clarity, and respect for my boundaries—even when it hurt him.

Seeing him in person, not as an idea in my head or a story my adoptive family told, but right there in front of me, changed everything. He was a man, not the myth I'd been fed. And though I didn't want to believe it, deep down, I sensed he was telling the truth. There was something about him, something so honest it didn't need any kind of backup or reinforcement. He simply was my father, standing there, reminding me of that. He listened, gently acknowledging my anger and pain but never pushing me to accept anything before I was ready.

In hindsight, I see how much strength it must have taken for him to stay calm. He was running for political office, yes, but I see now that this wasn't about his public image. No reporters or cameras could take away from the sincerity in his voice or the patience in his actions. There, standing before the world, he was there for me in the truest sense. He came to tell me that he was my father and that he loved me—simple, undeniable truths that I wasn't ready to accept at the time. But those words, though I didn't know it then, planted a seed that would later grow into my understanding of identity, of family, and of love.

As a child, I'd been told so many times that I wasn't worth loving, that I was merely an asset, a part of a paycheck. My adoptive family's lies and manipulation had warped my self-perception, making me question my value and doubt my own worth. Their lies made it seem as though I was a pawn in a game of wealth and control, stripped of a connection to my true family. This created a deep wound, a well of distrust that clouded every part of my young heart. But now, I understand that my father's visit was a moment where truth, quiet and unshakable, met those lies head-on.

My father taught me more during that short visit than I could have appreciated at the time. He showed me patience, empathy, and the strength to own one's mistakes and to stand by the truth no matter how painful it might be. He let me know that he loved me, but he also respected my feelings and my hurt. When I told him I wasn't ready, he didn't push. I could see that it wasn't easy for him—behind his calmness, there was a quiet pain, a sense of loss, as though he was losing something precious. Now, as an adult, I know that he was likely mourning the relationship we could have had, the time we'd missed, and the years that had passed by without us knowing one another.

In respecting my wishes, he taught me that love isn't about control or forcing things to fit a certain mold. Instead, love means letting go sometimes, trusting that one day the truth will come out and be enough. "What doesn't come out in the wash will come out in the rinse," as the old saying goes. And that's exactly how it's been for me—over time, the truth has washed away the lies, and I'm left with a clear sense of who I am and where I come from.

That moment, though it didn't sink in right away, became a foundation for my understanding of my own identity. For years, I struggled to make sense of who I was, feeling caught between two families, two worlds. I didn't belong entirely in one place or the other, carrying the weight of rejection, the ache of betrayal. My adoptive family's lies had convinced me that my father wanted something from me and that he didn't care about me as a person. But the reality was the opposite. He had shown up that day purely because he cared because he wanted me to know him and know the truth about my heritage.

My journey to self-acceptance and understanding my identity wasn't immediate, but it started in that room, with him standing before me, telling me the truth I needed to hear. Over time, I began to see that I wasn't just a pawn or an asset. I was a person with a story, with a father who had tried his best to be part of my life despite the odds and the lies that stood between us.

Now, as an adult, I've come to embrace my relationship with my father, not as a myth but as a real, imperfect bond. I hold onto the memory of dancing with him, my feet on his as we glided across the floor. He wasn't just a visitor in my life; he was my father, with all the complexities and depth that come with that role. Someday, when we meet again, I'll be able to stand beside him as the person I've grown into— strong, self-aware, and proud of my heritage.

As I look back, I feel a profound sense of gratitude. His actions, his words, and his steady presence, even when I couldn't accept them, laid a path for me to reclaim my story and stand in my truth. I've come to see that my identity isn't something given to me by someone else. It's something I had to fight for, to uncover piece by piece. My father's love, his patience, and his commitment to the truth have shaped who

I am, helping me to see beyond the lies and embrace the truth of who I am and where I come from.

Every challenge, every painful revelation, has been part of my journey toward self-acceptance. My father, in his wisdom and restraint, gave me the space to find my own way. And though I regret not accepting the truth sooner, I'm grateful to be here now, ready to embrace it fully, ready to step forward with pride in who I am and the family I come from.

Chapter 7: The Role of Faith and Forgiveness

When I think about the word "Islam," one thing comes to mind immediately: peace. Islam literally means "submission" or "surrender," and it often translates into the idea of submitting to peace. It's this message of peace that attracted me to Islam in the first place. This wasn't a religion I was raised in, but it was one I grew increasingly drawn to as I grew older and my curiosity about the world expanded. Something about it felt deep, genuine, and resonated with my heart.

Islam was different from anything I'd known before. Yet, each time I read or learned something new about it, I felt my heart soften, my mind open, and a sense of calmness settled in me. One of the first things I learned was that the name of God in Islam is "Allah." And while Allah is most often translated as "God," it also carries the idea of the "all-knowing" being, the source of wisdom, compassion, and understanding. This thought humbled me — to believe in something so much greater than myself was freeing. I found that faith didn't feel restrictive or controlling but instead offered me a sense of release and strength.

One of the fundamental concepts in Islam is seeking knowledge. Prophet Muhammad, peace be upon him, emphasized this in one of his sayings: "Seek knowledge from the cradle to the grave." That line was life-changing for me. I realized that Islam wasn't just about beliefs; it was about learning, growing, and continuously evolving as a person. I've held on to that ever since. Even today, I seek knowledge in every corner, from books to people, from nature to my own experiences.

As I continued my journey, I made a commitment to learn Arabic, the language of the Qur'an, which is Islam's holy book. Learning Arabic wasn't easy; it was a whole new alphabet, new sounds, and a different rhythm. But as I learned each word and each phrase, I felt a deeper connection. Arabic is a beautifully expressive language, and it has over **12 million words** — more than English, which has around **170,000 words**. Each word seemed to carry a unique emotion, a rich meaning that opened up the teachings of Islam in a new way for me.

Learning Arabic allowed me to read and understand the Qur'an directly, and it was here that I found teachings that spoke to me deeply. I read verses that encouraged kindness, forgiveness, and patience. The idea of forgiveness in Islam particularly moved me. I learned that forgiveness wasn't just about letting others off the hook but also about letting myself off the hook. I came to realize that forgiveness is more about freeing myself from carrying the weight of resentment and anger.

When I forgave, I could feel a new kind of freedom, a lightness. I could let go of the bitterness I once held, allowing me to focus on the present and future without letting the past hold me back. This journey through forgiveness brought a peace that felt rare, and I wanted that peace to be a part of every step I took.

One of the greatest gifts Islam gave me was a sense of discipline. Islam encourages believers to pray five times a day. At first, the idea of pausing five times throughout the day sounded challenging. But as I adapted, I realized it added a beautiful structure to my day. These moments of prayer weren't just about ritual; they were small breaks to reflect, to refocus, and to reconnect with my purpose. Studies have shown that **mindful moments and short breaks** throughout the day can improve focus and mental well-being, and I was experiencing exactly that.

Through this discipline, I felt more in control of my time, my goals, and my actions. I became better at managing my emotions, even in challenging moments, and more motivated to pursue my goals with a clear and peaceful mind. This new structure reminded me that I had a purpose. It gave me the confidence to stand out, not by becoming like everyone else, but by honoring my own journey and values.

My curiosity didn't stop with Islam; it became the beginning of a broader journey. Islam's encouragement of learning inspired me to dig into other areas of knowledge. I began exploring Egyptian history, with its ancient pyramids, pharaohs, and mysteries. Did you know that the Great Pyramid of Giza, which is over **4,500 years old**, is the only surviving wonder of the original Seven Wonders of the Ancient World? This civilization's dedication to knowledge and preservation fascinated me. The ancient Egyptians were mathematicians, architects, and thinkers ahead of their time, and studying their achievements reminded me of the power of human potential.

As I read about history and science, I also felt drawn to learn more languages. I taught myself Swahili, a language spoken by millions of people across Africa. Learning Swahili gave me a glimpse into different cultures, values, and perspectives. It showed me that knowledge connects us all. The phrase "Harambee," which means "let's pull together" in Swahili, captures this spirit of unity that I now hold close to.

Islam taught me that seeking knowledge isn't just about books and facts; it's about building bridges and understanding the world and its people.

For anyone curious about Islam, know that it's a journey of self-discovery and a reminder to focus on peace and growth. It encourages a balanced life, one where you strive to be a better person each day while contributing positively to the world. Islam showed me that peace begins from within, and once you have that peace, it radiates outward.

I hope this journey inspires you to keep learning and seeking your own truth, whatever path you choose.